BEHIND THE TIMES

BEHIND THE TIMES

THE DECLINE AND FALL
OF THE TWENTIETH-CENTURY
AVANT-GARDES

ERIC HOBSBAWM

THAMES AND HUDSON

*For Eva Neurath's
90th birthday*

The Walter Neurath Memorial Lectures, up to 1992, were given at Birkbeck College,
University of London, whose Governors and Master most generously
sponsored them for twenty-four years.

British Library Cataloguing-in-Publication Data
A catalogue record for this book is available from the British Library
ISBN 0-500-55031-X

Printed and bound in Italy by Editoriale Bortolazzi-Stei Srl

I never knew Walter Neurath except through his portrait by Oskar Kokoschka which still hangs in his and Eva's house in Highgate. However, there is no educated person in Britain with an interest in the arts who does not owe an enormous debt to the man who came from Vienna in 1938, who founded and directed the publishing house Thames and Hudson in 1949 and set it on the course which it still steers, thirty years after his death. What all such readers owe to Thames and Hudson books is incalculable. This lecture in his memory is a small personal thank you for great benefits.

The Walter Neurath Memorial Lectures were inaugurated in 1969 by my illustrious colleague at Birkbeck College, Nikolaus Pevsner. They have since been given by art historians of the eminence of Ernst Gombrich and John Pope-Hennessy. I can claim no such eminence in this field. I speak simply as a historian of the twentieth century, who has tried to reflect on the relations between the arts and society.

1 John Heartfield and
George Grosz:
Electromechanical Tatlin Shape,
1920.

The fundamental assumption behind the various movements of the avant-garde in the arts which dominate the past century was that relations between art and society had changed fundamentally, that old ways of looking at the world were inadequate and new ways must be found. This assumption was correct. What is more, the ways in which we look at and mentally apprehend the world *have* been revolutionized. However, and this is the core of my argument, in the visual arts this has not been achieved, and could not have been achieved, by the projects of the avant-garde.

Why, among all the arts, the visual ones have been particularly handicapped, I shall discuss in a little while. Anyway, they have patently failed. Indeed, after half a century of experiments in the revolutionary rethinking of art – say from 1905 to the middle 1960s –, the project was abandoned, leaving behind avant-gardes which became a subdepartment of marketing, or, if I may quote what I wrote in my history of the short twentieth century, *Age of Extremes*, 'the smell of impending death'. In that book I also considered whether this meant just the death of the avant-gardes or of the visual arts as conventionally recognized and practised since the Renaissance. However, I will leave the wider question aside here.

To avoid misunderstanding, let me at the outset say one thing. This essay is not about aesthetic judgments on the twentieth-century avant-gardes, whatever that means, or about assessing skill and talent. It is not about my own tastes and preferences in the arts. It is about the historic failure in our century of the sort of visual art which Moholy-Nagy of the Bauhaus once described as 'confined to picture-frame and pedestal'.[1]

We are talking about a double failure. It was a failure of 'modernity', a term which comes into use around the middle of the

nineteenth century, and which held programmatically that contemporary art must be, as Proudhon said of Courbet, 'an expression of the times'. Or, to put it in the words of the Vienna
Sezession: 'Der Zeit ihre Kunst, der Kunst ihre Freiheit' [Each age
needs its art, Art needs its freedom][2] – for the liberty of artists to do
what they and not necessarily anybody else want, was as central to
the avant-garde as its modernity. The demand for modernity
affected all arts equally: the art of each era had to be *different* from its
predecessors, which, in an age which assumed continuous progress,
seemed to suggest on the false analogy of science and technology
that each new way of expressing the times was likely to be *superior* to

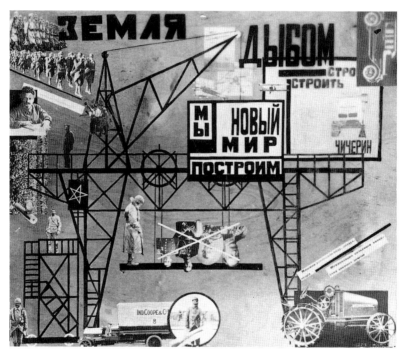

2 Liubov Popova: Photomontage for the set of Tretiakov's *The Earth in Turmoil*, 1923.

3 Fernand Léger: *The City*, 1919.

what went before; which is patently not always the case. There was, of course, no consensus about what 'expressing the times' meant, or on how to express them. Even when artists agreed that the century was essentially a 'machine age', or even – I am quoting Picabia in New York in 1915 – that 'through machinery art ought to find a most vivid expression'[3] or that 'the new art movements can exist only in a society that has absorbed the tempo of the big city, the metallic quality of industry' (Malevich),[4] most of the answers are trivial or rhetorical. Did it mean more to the Cubists than preferring, as Ortega y Gasset complained, the geometric scheme to the

4, 5 An artist who could change styles at will – the two personas of Victor Pasmore. On the left, *The Park*, 1947; on the right *Linear Motif*, 1960–61.

soft lines of living bodies? Or sticking artefacts of industrial society onto easel paintings? Did it mean more to the Dadaists, than the satirical construction by John Heartfield called *Electromechanical Tatlin Shape*, made out of industrial components, which they exhibited, inspired by news of a new 'machine art' of the Russian Constructivists?[5] Did it mean just making pictures inspired by machinery, as Léger did so splendidly? The Futurists were smart enough to leave real machines out and concentrate on trying to create the impression of rhythm and speed; the opposite of Jean Cocteau, who talked of the rhythm of machinery in terms of the metre and rhyme of poetry.[6] In short, the numerous ways of expressing machine-modernity in painting or non-utilitarian constructions had absolutely nothing in common except the word 'machine' and possibly, though not always, a preference for straight lines over undulating ones. There was no compelling logic to the new forms of expression, which is why varying schools and styles could coexist, none lasted, and the same artists could change styles like shirts. The 'modernity' lay in the changing times, not in the arts which tried to express them.

The second failure was much more acute in the visual arts than elsewhere: it was the increasingly evident technical inability of the main medium of painting since the Renaissance – the easel picture – to 'express the times', or indeed to compete with new ways of carrying out many of its traditional functions. The history of the visual avant-gardes in the present century is the struggle against technological obsolescence.

Could we also say that painting and sculpture found themselves at a disadvantage in another respect? They were the least important or prominent components in the great multiple or collective movement-filled presentations which have become increasingly typical of twentieth-century cultural experience: from grand opera at one pole to film, video and rock concert at the other. No one was more aware of this than the avant-gardes which, ever since Art Nouveau, and with impassioned conviction since the Futurists, believed in breaking down the walls between colour, sound, shape and words, that is in the unification of the arts. As in Wagner's *Gesamtkunstwerk,* music, word, gesture, lighting carry the action; the static image is background. Films depended on books from the start, and imported writers who had made a literary reputation – Faulkner, Hemingway – though rarely to good effect. The impact of twentieth-century painting on the movies (other than on specific avant-garde films) is limited: some expressionism in the Weimar cinema, the influence of Edward Hopper's pictures of American houses on Hollywood set designers. It is no accident that the index to the recent *Oxford History of World Cinema* contains a heading *music,* but none relevant to painting except *animation* (which, in turn, does not figure in Robert Hughes' *American Visions* ('the epic history of art in America'). Unlike literary writers and classical composers, no painter known to mainstream art history has ever been in the running for an Oscar. The only form of collective art in which the painter, and especially, since Diaghilev, the avant-garde painter, really acted as a partner rather than a subordinate, was the ballet.

However, apart from this possible disadvantage, what were the special difficulties of the visual arts?

Any study of the non-utilitarian visual arts in the twentieth century – I mean painting and sculpture – must start from the observation that they are a minority interest. In 1994 21% of people in this country had visited a museum or art gallery at least once in the last quarter, 60% read books at least once a week, 58% listened to records and tapes at least once a week, and almost all the 96% of televiewers presumably saw films or their equivalent regularly.[7] As for practising them, in 1974 only 4.4% of French people claimed to paint or sculpt as a hobby as against 15.4% who said they played a musical instrument.[8] The problems of painting and sculpture are, of course, rather different. The demand for pictures is essentially for private consumption. Public painting such as murals has been prominent only occasionally in our century, notably in Mexico. This has restricted the market for works of visual art, unless they are attached to something for which there is a larger public, such as record-sleeves, periodicals and book-jackets. Still, as the population grew and people became richer, there was no a priori reason for this market to shrink. As against this the demand for the *plastic* arts was public. Their problem was that the market for its major product collapsed in our century, namely the public monument and the decorated building or space, which modernist architecture rejected. Remember Adolf Loos' phrase: 'Ornament is Crime.' Since the peak era before 1914, when an average of about 35 new monuments

6 Monument to Gambetta that once stood outside the Louvre, Paris.

were erected in Paris every decade, there has actually been a holocaust of statuary: 75 disappeared from Paris during the war, and in doing so changed the face of the city.[9] The enormous demand for war memorials after 1918, the temporary rise of sculpture-happy dictatorships, have not halted the secular decline. So the crisis of the plastic arts is somewhat different from that of painting, and I will, reluctantly, say no more about them. Nor, indeed, except incidentally, about architecture, which has been largely immune to the problems that have beset the other visual arts.

But we must also start from another observation. More than any other form of creative art, the visual arts have suffered from technological obsolescence. They, and in particular painting, have been unable to come to terms with what Walter Benjamin called 'the age of technical reproducibility'. From the middle of the nine-teenth century – that is, from the time when we can recognize

7 A dismembered Stalin being consigned to oblivion in Budapest.

conscious movements of the avant-garde in painting,– though the word itself had not yet entered current discourse on the arts – they have been aware both of the competition of technology, in the form of the camera, and of their inability to survive this competition. A conservative critic of photography pointed out as early as 1850 that it must seriously jeopardize 'entire branches of art such as engravings, lithography, genre pictures and portraiture'.[10] Some sixty years later, the Italian Futurist Boccioni argued that contemporary art must be expressed in abstract terms, or rather by a spiritualization of the objective, because 'traditional representation has now been taken over by mechanical means' [– 'in luogo della riproduzione tradizionale ormai conquistata dai mezzi mec-canici'][11]. Dada, or so at least Wieland Herzfelde proclaimed, would not try to compete with the camera, or even try to be a camera with soul, like the Impressionists, trusting as they had done to the least reliable of lenses, the human eye.[12] Jackson Pollock, in 1950, said art had to express feelings, because making pictures of things was now done with cameras.[13] Similar examples could be quoted from almost any decade of the century up to the present. As the president of the Pompidou Centre observed in 1998: 'The twentieth century belongs to photography, not painting.'[14]

Statements of this kind are familiar to everyone who has even glanced at the literature of the arts – at least in the western tradition since the Renaissance – since they can plainly not apply to arts which are not concerned with mimesis or other modes of repre-sentation, or which pursue other ends. There is obvious truth in them. However, there is, in my view, another equally powerful reason for the losing battle the traditional visual arts have waged against technology in our century. It is the mode of production to which the visual artist was committed, and from which he or she found it difficult or even impossible to escape. This was the produc-tion by manual labour of unique works, which could not be literally copied except by the same method. Indeed, the ideal work of art is deemed to be completely uncopiable, since its uniqueness is authenticated by signature and provenance. There was, of course, much potential, including much economic potential, in works designed for technical reproduction, but the one-off product, ascribable to one and only one maker, remained the foundation of the status of high-class visual art and the high-status 'artist', as distinct from the journeyman artisan or 'hack'. And avant-garde painters also insisted on their special status as artists. Until almost this day the stature of painters has tended to be proportional to the size of the frames surrounding their pictures. Such a mode of production belongs typically to a society of patronage or of small groups competing in conspicuous expenditure, and indeed these are still the foundation of the really lucrative art trade. But it is profoundly unsuited to an economy which relies on the demand not of single individuals or a few dozens or scores, but of thousands or even millions; in short, to the mass economy of this century.

None of the other arts suffered so severely from this problem. Architecture, as we know, continues as an art to rely on patronage, which is why it continues happily to produce jumbo-sized one-off prodigies, with or without modern technology. For obvious reasons it is also immune to forgery, the bane of painting. The arts of the stage, though technically pretty antediluvian, have by their nature relied on repeated performance before a large public, that is to say on reproducibility. The same is true of music even before the modern technology of sound reproduction made it accessible beyond the range of mouth-to-ear communication. The standard version of the musical work is expressed in a code of symbols whose essential function is to make possible repeated performance. Of course *invariant* repetition was neither possible nor highly appreciated in these arts, before the twentieth century, when accurate mechanical reproduction became feasible. Literature,

8 Raoul Hausmann: *Phonetic poem-poster*, 1918.

finally, had solved the problem of art in the age of reproducibility centuries ago. Printing emancipated it from the calligraphers and their underclass, the copyists. The brilliant invention of the pocket-sized bound volume in the sixteenth century gave it the universally portable and multipliable form which has so far seen off all the challenges of modern technology which were supposed to replace the book – film, radio, television, video, audio-book, and, except for special purposes, CD-Rom and computer-screen.

The crisis of the visual arts is therefore different in kind from the twentieth-century crisis so far undergone by the other arts. Literature never gave up the traditional use of language, or even, in poetry, the constraints of metre. The brief and isolated experiments to break with these, like *Finnegans Wake*, remain peripheral, or are not treated as literature at all, like the Dada 'phonetic poem-poster'

18

OFFEAHBDC BDQ꜡„qjyE!

of the Dadaist Raoul Hausmann. Here modernist revolution was compatible with technical continuity. In music the avant⁄garde of composers broke more dramatically with the nineteenth⁄century idiom, but the bulk of the musical public remained loyal to the classics, supplemented by assimilated nineteenth⁄century post⁄ Wagnerian innovators. They retained and still retain a virtual monopoly of the popular performance repertoire. This therefore comes almost entirely from the graveyard. Only in the visual arts, and especially in painting, did the then conventional form of mimesis, the salon art of the nineteenth century. virtually disappear from sight, as witness the almost vertical fall in its price on the art market between the wars. Nor, in spite of all efforts of the art⁄ traders, has it been rehabilitated even today. The good news for avant⁄garde painting was therefore that it was the only live game in town. The bad news was, that the public didn't like it. Abstract painting did not begin to sell at serious prices until the Cold War

9 Edvard Munch: *The Scream*, 1893. Here naturalism is retained but manipulated and distorted in order to express emotion.

when, by the way, it benefited from Hitler and Stalin's hostility to it. It therefore became a sort of official art of the Free World against Totalitarianism – a curious destiny for the enemies of bourgeois convention.

So long as the essence of traditional visual art, namely representation, was not abandoned, this was not a major problem. In fact, until the end of the nineteenth century both musical and visual avant-gardes – Impressionists, Symbolists, Post-Impressionists, Art Nouveau and the like – extended rather than abandoned the old language, as well as widening the range of subjects that could be treated by artists. Paradoxically, here the competition of photography proved stimulating. Painters still had exclusive rights to colour, and it is hardly an accident that, from the Impressionists through the Fauves, colour becomes increasingly vivid, if not strident. They also seemed to retain the monopoly of 'express-

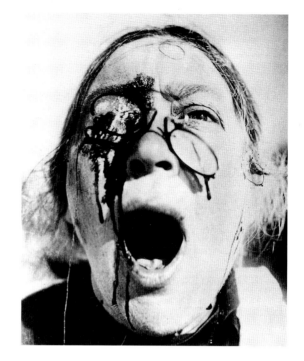

10 A still from the Odessa steps sequence of Sergei Eisenstein's *Battleship Potemkin*, 1925, where the cinema achieves the same emotional intensity through naturalistic means.

ionism' in the most general sense, and thus exploited the ability to infuse reality with emotion – all the more powerfully once the bonds of naturalism were relaxed, as witness Van Gogh and Munch. Actually, film technology was later to demonstrate an ability to compete.

Again, artists could still try, or at least claim, to get closer to perceived reality than the machine could, by appealing to science against technology. At least that is what artists like Cézanne, Seurat and Pissarro said or propagandists like Zola or Apollinaire said for them.[15] The drawback of this procedure was that it removed painting from what the eye saw – that is the physical perception of ever-changing light on objects, or the relations of planes and shapes or geological structure – to the conventional codes of what skies, trees, people were *supposed* to look like. Still, until the Cubists, the distance was not too great: the avant-gardes of the late nineteenth

22

11, 12 In popularity ratings, a work such as Van Gogh's *Sunflowers* (1888) remains more accessible to a wider public than a Cubist picture like Braque's *Man with Guitar* (1911–12), which needs to be explained before it is understood.

century, up to and including Post-Impressionism, have become part of the accepted corpus of art. In fact, their artists acquired genuine mass popularity, insofar as this term applies to painting. In Bourdieu's enquiry on French taste in the 1970s, Renoir and Van Gogh emerge as by far the most popular artists at all socio-professional levels, except academics and 'producteurs artistiques'. (There Goya and Brueghel beat Renoir into fourth place.[16]) The real break between public and artist came with the new century. In Bourdieu's sample, for instance, Van Gogh remained about four times as popular as Braque even among the most highbrow group, in spite of the social cachet of abstract art, which 43 percent of the group claimed to like. For every one who chose the eminent and thoroughly French Cubist in the so-called 'popular classes', 10 chose the Dutchman; in the middle classes 7 did so, and even in the upper classes Van Gogh beat Braque easily by 5 to 1.

23

Why, between say 1905 and 1914, the avant-garde deliberately broke this continuity with the past is a question I can't answer adequately. But once it had done so, it was necessarily on the way to nowhere. What could painting do once it abandoned the traditional language of representation, or moved sufficiently far from its conventional idiom to make it incomprehensible? What could it communicate? Where was the new art going? The half-century from the Fauves to Pop Art was filled with desperate attempts to answer this question by means of an endless succession of new styles and their associated and often impenetrable manifestoes. Contrary to the conventional belief, they had nothing in common except the conviction that it was important to be an artist and, once representation was left to cameras, that anything was legitimate as art, so long as the artist claimed it as a personal creation. Except for brief periods it is not even possible to define a general trend, such as one away from representation to abstraction, or from content to form and colour. *Neue Sachlichkeit* and Surrealism did not come before but after Cubism. A perceptive critic has said of Jackson

13 Jackson Pollock: *Autumn Rhythm*, 1950.

24

14, 15 Modern art feeding on the art of the past: a plate from Goya's *Disasters of War* (A heroic feat! With the dead!), c.1810, exploited, or parodied, by Jake and Dinos Chapman's *Great Deeds against the Dead*, 1994.

Pollock, the Abstract Expressionist par excellence, that 'perhaps if he had lived to seventy . . . he would now be seen as a basically imagistic artist who had one abstract phase in his early middle age.'[17]

This uncertainty gives the history of the avant-gardes an air of particular desperation. They were constantly torn between the conviction that there could be no future to the art of the past – even yesterday's past, or even to any kind of art in the old definition – and the conviction that what they were doing in the old social role of 'artists' and 'geniuses' was important, and rooted in the great tradition of the past. The Cubists very naturally, but to Marinetti's displeasure, 'adore the traditionalism of Poussin, Ingres and Corot'.[18] More absurdly, the late Yves Klein, who coloured all his canvases and other objects a uniform blue in the manner of a house-painter, may be regarded as a reductio ad absurdum of the artist's activity, but he justified this by saying that the intention of Giotto and Cimabue had been 'monochromatic'.[19] The recent 'Sensation' exhibition catalogue tried to mobilize the status of Géricault, Manet, Goya and Bosch in favour of the likes of Jake and Dinos Chapman.

16 Piet Mondrian: *Trafalgar Square*, 1939–43.

Nevertheless, the new freedom enormously increased the range of what could be done in the visual arts. It was both inspiring and liberating, especially for people who believed an unprecedented century needed to be expressed in unprecedented ways. It is almost impossible not to share the sheer excitement and exhilaration radiated by such records of an heroic age in the arts as the great *Berlin-Moskau* exhibition of 1996–7. Nevertheless, it could not conceal two things. First, much less could be communicated in the impoverished new languages of painting than in the old ones. This actually made it harder, or even impossible, to 'express the times' in a communicable way. Anything more than exercises in 'significant form' – the famous Bloomsbury phrase – or than the expression of subjective feeling, needed subtitles and commentators more than ever. That is to say it needed words, which still had conventional meanings. As a poet W.B. Yeats had no trouble in communicating his odd and somewhat esoteric views, but without words it is impossible to discover in Mondrian and Kandinsky that these artists wished to express very strongly held and equally eccentric views about the world. Second, the new century could be much more effectively expressed by its own novel media. In short, whatever the avant-garde tried to do was either impossible or done better in some other medium. For this reason most of the revolutionary claims of the avant-garde were rhetoric or metaphor.

Let us consider Cubism, the avant-garde which has been described, more than once, as 'the most revolutionary and influential of the twentieth century'.[20] This may be true as far as other painters are concerned, at least for the period from 1907 to the First World War; though I think that, so far as the arts as a whole are concerned, Surrealism was to be more influential, possibly because its inspiration was not primarily visual. And yet, was it Cubism that revolutionized the way we all – and not just professional painters – see the world? For instance, Cubism claimed to

17 Alexander Rodchenko: Portrait of the artist Alexander Svenchenko, 1924, using double exposure to achieve a multidimensional effect.

18 Pablo Picasso: Cubist portrait of Daniel-Henry Kahnweiler, 1910.

present different aspects of objects simultaneously giving, as it were, a multidimensional view of what would otherwise be, say, a still life or the human face. (Actually, when we look at the paintings of the analytical phase of Cubism, we still have to be told that this is what they are supposed to do.) Yet almost simultaneously with Cubism, that is from 1907 on, the movies began to develop those techniques of multiple perspective, varying focus and tricks of cutting, which really familiarized a huge public – indeed all of us – with apprehending reality through simultaneous, or almost simultaneous, perceptions of its different aspects; and this without the need for commentary. Moreover, even when the inspiration was directly Cubist, as, presumably, in Rodchenko's photo, it is the photograph which, plainly, communicates the sense of the innovation more effectively than a comparable painting by Picasso. That is why photomontage was to prove so powerful a tool for propaganda. I am not, of course, comparing the aesthetic value of the Picasso and the Rodchenko.

19 Poster for *Gone with the Wind*, 1939.

In short, it is impossible to deny that the real revolution in the twentieth-century arts was achieved not by the avant-gardes of modernism, but outside the range of the area formally recognized as 'art'. It was achieved by the combined logic of technology and the mass market, that is to say the democratization of aesthetic consumption. And chiefly, of course, by the cinema, child of photography and the central art of the twentieth century. Picasso's *Guernica* is incomparably more impressive as art, but, speaking technically, Selznick's *Gone with the Wind* is a more revolutionary work. For that matter Disney's animations, however inferior to the austere beauty of Mondrian, were both more revolutionary than oil-painting and better at passing on their message. Advertisements and movies, developed by hucksters, hacks and technicians, not only drenched everyday life in aesthetic experience, but converted the masses to daring innovations in visual perception, which left the

30

20 Pablo Picasso: detail from *Guernica*, 1937.

21 Giacomo Balla: *Abstract Speed*, 1913.

revolutionaries of the easel far behind, isolated and largely irrelevant. A camera on a footplate can communicate the sensation of speed better than a Futurist canvas by Balla. The point about the real revolutionary arts is that they were accepted by the masses because they *had* to communicate with them. Only in avant-garde art was the medium the message. In real life, the medium was revolutionized for the sake of the message.

It took the triumph of modern consumer society in the 1950s to make the avant-gardes recognize this. Once they did so their justification was gone.

The avant-garde schools since the 1960s – since Pop Art – were no longer in the business of revolutionizing art, but of declaring its bankruptcy. Hence the curious reversion to conceptual art and Dadaism. In the original versions of 1914 and after, these were not supposed to be ways of revolutionizing art but of abolishing it, or at least declaring its irrelevance, for instance by painting a moustache on the Mona Lisa and treating a bicycle wheel as a 'work of art' as Marcel Duchamp did. When the public didn't get the point, he exhibited his urinal with an invented artist's signature. Duchamp was lucky enough to do this in New York, where he became a great name, and not in Paris, where he was just one very bright intellectual joker among many, and had no standing as an artist. (As Cartier-Bresson says: he was 'not a good artist at all'.) Dada was serious even in its most desperate jokes: nothing cool, ironic and shoulder-shrugging about it. It wanted to destroy art together with the bourgeoisie, as part of the world which had brought about the Great War. Dada did not accept the world. When George Grosz moved to the USA and there found a world he did not abominate, he lost his power as an artist.

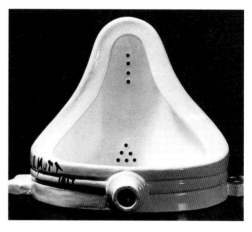

22, 23 Dada subverts art.
Left: poster for Dada fair.
Above: Marcel Duchamp's
Urinal, 1917.

34

24, 25 George Grosz before and after moving to America. Left: *Eva*, 1918, from
Ecce Homo. Above: *Study in Texture*, 1939.

Warhol and the Pop Artists did not want to destroy or revolu-tionize anything, let alone any world. On the contrary, they accepted, even liked it. They simply recognized that there was no longer a place for traditional artist-produced visual art in the consumer society, except, of course, as a way of earning money. A real world, flooding every waking hour with a chaos of sounds, images, symbols, presumptions of a common experience, had put art as a special activity out of business. Warhol's significance – I might even say the greatness of this strange and disagreeable figure – lies in the consistency of his refusal to do anything but make himself the passive, accepting, conduit for the world experienced through media-saturation. Nothing is shaped. There are no winks and nudges, no ironies, no sentimentality, no ostensible commentary at all, except by implication in the choice of his mechanically repeated icons – Mao, Marilyn, Campbell's Soup tins – and perhaps in his deep preoccupation with death. Paradoxically, in the ensemble of this troubling oeuvre – though not in any single work – we actually come closer to an 'expression of the times' in which contemporary Americans lived. But it was not achieved by creating works of art in the traditional sense.

Effectively, since then there has been nothing left for avant-garde painting to do. Dadaism has returned, but this time not as a desper-ate protest against an intolerable world, but just as the old Dadaist gift for publicity stunts. Easel painting itself is in retreat. Conceptualism is the flavour of the day, because it is easy and it is something that even unskilled humans can do and camcorders can't, namely having ideas, especially if they need not be good or interesting ideas. I note in passing that actual painting disappeared from this year's Turner Prize altogether.

So, has the history of the twentieth-century avant-gardes then been entirely esoteric? Have its effects been entirely confined to a self-contained art-world? Did they entirely fail in their project of

26 Andy Warhol: *Marilyn*, 1967. Unlike Dada, Pop Art accepts the world, and indeed 'expresses the time' more faithfully than the avant-gardes.

expressing and transforming the twentieth century? Not entirely.

There was a way in which they could break with the crippling tradition of art as the production of irreproducible artefacts by artists pleasing only themselves. It was by recognizing the logic of life and production in industrial society. For, of course, industrial society could recognize the need for aesthetic as well as technical innovation, if only because production and marketing/propaganda needed both. 'Modernist' criteria had practical value for industrial design and mechanized mass production. Avant-garde techniques

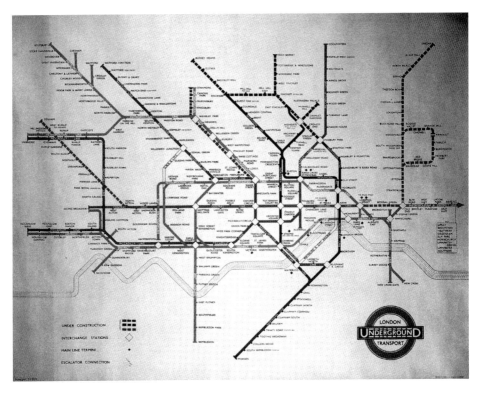

27 H.C. Beck's map of the London Underground system, 1939 – technology and art in the service of rational communication.

28 Simon Patterson: *The Great Bear*, 1992.

were effective in advertising. To the extent that these ideas came from the avant-gardes of the early twentieth century we live in a visual environment shaped by them. Often they did, though not always and necessarily. The most original work of avant-garde art in Britain between the wars was not produced as a work of art at all, but as an efficient technical solution for a problem of how to present information: it is the map of the London underground system. Incidentally, the bankruptcy of the avant-garde is vividly demonstrated in the pointless adaptation of this by Simon Patterson in this year's 'Sensation' show.

39

One avant-garde tradition did make the junction between the nineteenth- and twentieth-century worlds. This was the tradition which – as Nikolaus Pevsner rightly recognized[21] – led from William Morris, Arts-and-Crafts and Art Nouveau to the Bauhaus, at least once it had shaken off the original hostility to industrial production, engineering and distribution. John Willett has shown how the Bauhaus did this in the early 1920s. The strength of this tradition – reinforced as it was in the Bauhaus by Russian Constructivism – was that it was fuelled not by the concerns of artists as individual genius-creators with esoteric technical problems, but as builders of a better society. As Moholy-Nagy, an exile from Hungary after the defeat of the shortlived Hungarian Soviet republic, put it: 'Constructivism is the socialism of vision.' This kind of post-1917 avant-garde leaped back across the non-political or even anti-political avant-gardes of 1905–1914 to the socially committed movements of the 1880s and early 1890s. New art was once again inseparable from building a new, or at least an improved society. Its impetus was social as well as aesthetic. Hence the centrality of building – the German word which gave the Bauhaus its name – to this project.

Here the aesthetics of the 'machine age' made more than rhetorical sense. In the 1920s the programme for changing the way humans lived that appealed to the artists who could contribute directly to this object tended to be a combination of public planning and technological utopia. It was a marriage between Henry Ford, who wanted to provide cars where there had been none, and the aspirations of socialist municipalities to provide bath-rooms where there had been none. Both in their different ways claimed to be experts who knew best; both aimed at universal improvement; neither gave priority to personal choice ('You can have my cars in any colour so long as it's black'). Houses and even cities, like the cars which Le Corbusier regarded as the model for

40

29 The efficient production-line in the
home: film stills from *Femme dans la Cuisine*.

constructing houses[22] were conceived as products of the universal logic of industrial production. The basic principle of the 'machine age' could be applied to human environments and human dwellings ('a machine for living in') by finding the solution for the combined problem of optimising the human use of limited space, ergonomics and cost-effectiveness. It was a good ideal, which made the lives of a lot of people better, even if the utopian aspirations of its Cité Radieuse belong to an era, even in the world's rich countries, of modest needs and restricted means, far from the super-abundance, and hence the possible consumer choice, of our times.

Nevertheless, as even the Bauhaus discovered, changing society is more than schools of art and design alone can achieve. And it was not achieved. Let me conclude by quoting the last and sad sentences of Paul Klee's lecture 'On Modern Art', given not far from the Bauhaus, then at its creative peak (1924): 'We don't have the support of a people. But we are looking for a people. That is how we began, over there at the Bauhaus. We started with a community to which we gave all we had. We can't do more than that.'[23] And it wasn't enough.

NOTES
LIST OF ILLUSTRATIONS

NOTES

1 Cited in John Willett, *The New Sobriety: Art and Politics in the Weimar Period 1917–1933*, London, 1978, p. 76.

2 Cited in Linda Nochlin ed. *Realism and Tradition in Art*, Englewood Cliffs, 1996, p. 53.

3 'French Artists Spur on American Art' in *New York Tribune* 24 October 1915.

4 Cited in L. Brion-Guerry ed. *L'Année 1913: Les formes esthétiques de l'oeuvre d'art à la veille de la première guerre mondiale*, Paris, 1971, p. 89, n. 34.

5 Catalogue of Exhibition *Berlin-Moskau 1900–1950*, pp. 118 (fig 1), 120–21.

6 Brion-Guerry *op cit.* p. 86, n. 27.

7 Economist, *Pocket Britain in Figures: 1997 Edition*, pp. 194, 195.

8 T. Zeldin, *France 1848–1945*, vol II, p. 446.

9 Pierre Nora ed. *Les lieux de mémoire II: La Nation* vol. III, p. 256.

10 Gisèle Freund, *Photographie und bürgerliche Gesellschaft*, Munich, 1968, p. 92.

11 Cited in L. Brion-Guerry ed. *op. cit*, p. 92.

12 Catalogue *Paris-Berlin.1900-1933* (Pompidou Centre 1978),pp. 170–71.

13 Cited in C. Harrison and P. Wood eds. *Art in Theory 1900–1990*, Oxford, 1992, p. 576.

14 Cited in Suzy Menkes, 'Man Ray, Designer behind the Camera' *International Herald Tribune*, May 5 1998, p. 12.

15 T. Zeldin *France 1848–1945* vol II, pp. 480, 481.

16 P. Bourdieu, *La Distinction: critique sociale du jugement*, Paris, 1979, p. 615. Respondents were asked to choose among the following artists: Raphael, Buffet, Utrillo, Vlaminck, Watteau, Renoir, Van Gogh, Dali, Braque, Goya, Brueghel, Kandinsky.

17 Robert Hughes, *American Visions*, pp. 487–88.

18 Brion-Guerry *op cit.* p. 297, n. 29.

19 C. Harrison and P. Wood eds, *op cit.*, p. 804.

20 Alan Bullock, Oliver Stallybrass eds. *The Fontana Dictionary of Modern Thought*, London, 1977, entry: 'Cubism'.

21 Nikolaus Pevsner, *Pioneers of Modern Design: From William Morris to Walter Gropius*, London, 1991 edition.

22 Brion-Guerry, *op cit.*, p. 86, n. 27.

23 Paul Klee, *Uber die moderne Kunst*, Bern, 1945, p. 53.

LIST OF ILLUSTRATIONS

1. John Heartfield and George Grosz *Electromechanical Tatlin Shape* 1920/1988 reconstruction by Michael Sellmann H 130 (51 ⅛). Landesmuseum Berlinische Galerie, Berlin. © DACS 1999

2. Liubov Popova, photomontage for the set of Tretiakov's *The Earth in Turmoil* 1923.

3. Fernand Léger *The City* 1919. Oil on canvas 231 x 298.5 (91 x 117 ½). Philadelphia Museum of Art. A.E. Gallatin Collection. © ADAGP, Paris and DACS, London 1999

4. Victor Pasmore *The Park* 1947. Oil on canvas 110 x 78.5 (43 ¼ x 30 ⅞). Sheffield City Art Galleries

5. Victor Pasmore *Linear Motif in Black and White* 1960⁄61. Mixed media 121.9 x 121.9 (48 x 48). Tate Gallery, London

6. Monument to Gambetta. Photo Roger ⁄Viollet, Paris

7. Monument to Stalin. © Ferdinando Scianna/Magnum Photos

8. Raoul Hausmann *Phonetic poem⁄ poster* 1918. Ink, paper and cardboard 33 x 48 (13 x 19). Musée National d'Art Moderne, Paris. © ADAGP, Paris and DACS, London 1999

9. Edvard Munch *The Scream* 1893. Oil on board 91 x 73.5 (35 ⅞ x 29). Nasjonalgalleriet, Oslo. © Munch Museum /Munch⁄Ellingsen Group/BONO, Oslo/DACS, London 1999

10. A still from *Battleship Potemkin* 1925. Photo BFI Stills, Posters & Designs, London

11. Vincent van Gogh *Sunflowers* 1888. Oil on canvas 93 x 73 (36 ⅝ x 28 ¾). National Gallery, London

12. Georges Braque *Man with a Guitar* 1911–12. Oil on canvas 116.2 x 80.9 (45 ¾ x 31 ⅞). The Museum of Modern Art, New York. Acquired through the Lillie P. Bliss Bequest, 1945. Photograph © 1998 The Museum of Modern Art, New York. © ADAGP, Paris and DACS, London 1999

13. Jackson Pollock *Autumn Rhythm* 1950. Oil on canvas 262 x 550 (103 ⅛ x 216 ½). The Metropolitan Museum of Art, New York.

14. Goya *A heroic feat! With the dead !* from the *Disasters of War* series c.1810. Etching, lavis and drypoint 15.6 x 20.8 (6 ⅛ x 8 ⅛). Collection of the Fundación Juan March, Madrid

15. Jake and Dinos Chapman *Great Deeds against the Dead* 1994. Mixed media with plinth 277 x 244 x 152 (109 x 96 x 59 ⅞). Saatchi Collection, London

16. Piet Mondrian *Trafalgar Square* 1939–43. Oil on canvas 145.2 x 120 (57 ¼ x 47 ¼). The Museum of Modern Art, New York. Gift of Mr. and Mrs. William A. M. Burden. Photograph © 1998 The Museum of Modern Art, New York. © 1999 Mondrian/Holtzman Trust, c/o Beeldrecht, Amsterdam, Holland/DACS, London

17. Alexander Rodchenko, photograph of the artist Alexander Svenchenko 1924. © DACS 1999

18. Pablo Picasso *Portrait of Daniel-Henry Kahnweiler* 1910. Oil on canvas 100.6 x 72.8 (39 ½ x 28 ⅝).

The Art Institute of Chicago. Gift of Mrs. Gilbert W. Chapman in memory of Charles B. Goodspeed. © Succession Picasso/DACS 1999

19. Poster for *Gone with the Wind* 1939. Photo Ronald Grant Archive, London

20. Pablo Picasso *Guernica* 1937 (detail). Oil on canvas 350.5 x 782.3 (11' 6" x 25' 8"). Museo del Prado, Madrid. © Succession Picasso/DACS 1999

21. Giacomo Balla *Abstract Speed* 1913. Oil on canvas 76.5 x 108 (30 ⅛ x 42 ½). Private collection. © DACS 1999

22. Photograph of Dada fair.

23. Marcel Duchamp *Urinal* 1917. Original destroyed. © ADAGP, Paris and DACS, London 1999

24. George Grosz *Eva* 1918. Pen and ink, plate 51 from *Ecce Homo*. © DACS 1999

25. George Grosz *Study in Texture* 1939. Chalk and sanguine 63.5 x 48.3 (25 x 19). Private collection. © DACS 1999

26. Andy Warhol *Marilyn* 1967.
    Screenprint 91.4 x 91.4 (36 x 36).
    Frederick R. Weismann Art
    Foundation, Los Angeles.
    © The Andy Warhol Foundation
    for the Visual Arts, Inc./DACS,
    London 1999

27. H.C. Beck, map of the London
    Underground system 1939.

© London Transport Museum

28. Simon Patterson *The Great Bear*
    1992. Lithographic print 109 x
    134.8 x 5 (43 ⅝ x 53 x 2). Courtesy
    Lisson Gallery, London. Photo
    John Riddy

29. Film stills from *Femme dans la Cuisine.*
    Cinémathèque Française, Paris

48